THE OFFICIAL **RSPCA** PET GUIDE

Care for your

Tropical Fish

This book is to be returned on or before the last date stamped below.

WITHDRAWN
FROM STOCK

Record Card

photograph

Record sheet for your own aquarium

Species   Dates acquired

_____   _____

_____   _____

_____   _____

_____   Feeding notes

_____   _____

_____   _____

_____   _____

Plant varieties   Breeding record (if applicable)

_____   _____

_____   _____

_____   Health record

_____   _____

_____   _____

Veterinary surgeon's name   Surgery hours

Practice address   Tel. no.

Choosing Tropical Fish

Keeping and breeding fish has been a favourite hobby of the Chinese and Japanese for over two thousand years. However, keeping tropical fish in heated glass tanks is a relatively recent interest. The first public aquarium in the world was opened in England in 1852, in the Zoological Gardens in Regent's Park, London, and since then, keeping and breeding tropical fish has increased in popularity enormously.

Tropical fish can be divided into two categories: freshwater and marine fish. This book is concerned only with freshwater tropical fish. The requirements for marine fish tend to be complex and demand considerable expertise, as well as more time, effort and money than the newcomer to fish keeping will wish to expend.

That said, keeping freshwater fish as pets still requires certain basic commitments on the part of the owner. Fish are living creatures and although they cannot show their feelings as demonstratively as cats or dogs, they still need to be well looked after if they are to thrive. Do remember, if you are going away on holiday, for example, to make arrangements for someone else to look after your fish.

Remember, too, that they are totally dependent on the environment that you create for them. It is essential, therefore, that you set up your aquarium as carefully as you possibly can, and you must make sure that you provide conditions which are as close as possible to the fishes' natural environments. Some fish are shy and nocturnal, preferring to hide away amidst rocks and plants, while others like to sport and shoal in open water without plants.

Small, brightly coloured tropical freshwater fish can be readily found in aquarist shops, with some hundreds of different species commonly available. Given time for investigation, you should be able to discover combinations of colour and types that will not only make your aquarium a source of living interest and delight, but also ensure a congenial and healthy environment for the fish.

Biology

Scales   Externally, the body of the fish is covered with small bony plates – scales – which are themselves covered with a delicate layer of skin (although this is usually too thin to be seen without a microscope) that enlarges the scales as the fish grows. On top of this is a layer of mucus with bactericidal properties. The scales can only protect the fish by growing. If the delicate skin is damaged, growth is affected, so the fish's well-being is put at risk. For this reason extreme care must be taken when handling fish – better still, try not to handle them at all if possible. If too much mucus is removed by handling, bacteria can get into the skin and set up an infection; if too much skin is removed, the scales cannot grow; if the scales cannot grow, the fish can lose body fluids or become infected and die.

Eyes   Fish have no eyelids, so those kept in an aquarium need to be shaded from direct sunshine.

Gills   Most fish breathe by taking in water through the mouth, which then closes, the muscles squeezing the water out through slits in the side of the throat. The bars between the slits are lined with delicate blood-filled filaments (gill filaments), which act like our lungs. They pick up oxygen from the water and remove the carbon dioxide from the fish's blood. The gills nestle below a large protective plate just behind the head, which is called the gill cover, or operculum.

Fins   Fins are the most conspicuous features of a fish and are of great help in determining to which group of fishes your specimen belongs. As well as having locomotory functions, they can serve other purposes, as described here.

Pectoral fins   Just behind the operculum are the pectoral fins, which are the fish's equivalent of arms. Like the pelvic fins, they help the fish to brake and steer.

Dorsal fin   This fin may have spiny rays in the front or may be made up entirely of soft rays. It acts as a keel to stabilize the fish and, if brightly marked, may be rather like a signalling flag, helping to keep shoals together. It can also be used to 'warn' other species.

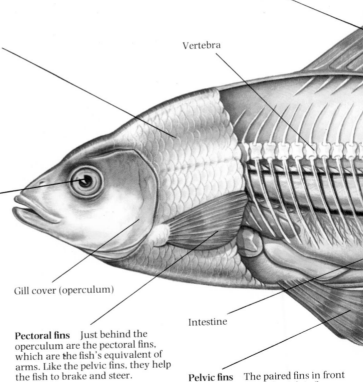

Vertebra

Gill cover (operculum)

Intestine

Pelvic fins   The paired fins in front of the anal fin are the pelvic fins. These help with braking and steering.

Swim bladder Many fish (indeed most you are likely to encounter) have a large gas- or air-filled sac variously called the swim bladder, gas bladder or air bladder. This is not usually used for breathing, but acts as a buoyancy chamber to keep the fish at the required depth in the water without effort. The fish uses its swim bladder to make itself neutrally buoyant.

Adipose fin Some fishes (characins and catfishes) have a small fatty fin called the adipose fin. No-one yet knows its precise function, but it will help you to identify an aquarium fish as a catfish or characin.

Muscle segment

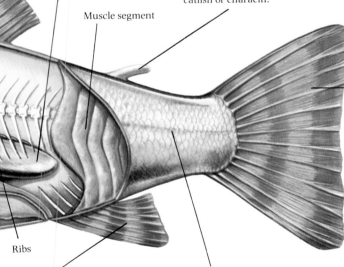

Caudal fin At the end of the body is the caudal or tail fin, which can be one of a variety of shapes. In the male swordtail the lower rays of the caudal fin are elongated into the colourful sword that gives these species their common name. The tail imparts the thrust of the side-to-side body movements which make the fish go forwards.

Ribs

Anal fin On the underside of the body, in front of the lower lobe of the caudal fin and just behind the anus, is the anal fin. Like the dorsal fin, it acts as a stabilizer, except in the males of live-bearing species where it is used in reproduction. For example, in fishes like guppies, platies, mollies, swordtails, etc., the anal fin of the male is modified into a rod-like structure to transfer the sperm to the female.

Lateral line Running down the side of many fish is a line, called the lateral line, which is formed by a series of pores in a row of scales. The pores lead to a canal with pressure-sensitive organs. The lateral line system acts like a sense of 'distant touch', which can alert the fish to obstacles and dangers.

How to Select Tropical Fish

Investigate before you buy
Because different species require different conditions, you need to know exactly what you want, and what their requirements are, before you decide which to buy. Moreover, unless you are quite sure you have a male and female of the same species you will never, of course, get them to breed.

It's also important to remember that some fish grow to be much bigger than others (so you will want fewer of them); some large fish will eat smaller ones (quickly reducing your fish population); and the males of certain species will fight endlessly if living together in an aquarium. Some fish prefer to live in small groups, while others are territorial and will threaten the other fish in the tank. Obviously, the larger the aquarium, the greater the number of species of fish you can keep.

If you are a beginner, it is probably best to start with those fish which are the easiest to keep and the least expensive to buy.

Choose a selection of fish
When you come to pick fish for your aquarium, it's generally a good idea to choose a selection which have different roles to play and which live at varying levels of the tank, thereby maximizing the available space in it.

Hatchet fish (*Gasteropelecus sternicla*): surface fish

Glowlight tetra (*Hemmigrammus erythrozonus*): middlewater fish

Broadly speaking, the tank can be divided into three levels: surface, middlewater and bottom. To obtain both an aesthetic and an 'ecological' balance, fish should be chosen to inhabit these three areas.

Know your fish families
One further point on choosing fish: try not to be too bewildered by the names and varieties. Many fish are sold under a 'common' name rather than the internationally accepted scientific name. For instance, rather than referring to *Xenocara dolichoptera* (a very distinctive catfish), you will find many dealers use names like 'flag cat', 'blue chin' or 'Guyanan blue fin'. However, the common names can actually lead to a lot of confusion, so it is really easier in the long run to use the scientific names.

Essentially, the scientific name consists of a genus name, or 'surname', which is put first, and a descriptive name, which follows. Take the 'red-tailed black shark', for example (deliberately chosen because it is *not* a shark): its scientific name is *Labeo bicolor*. *Labeo* is the name of the genus and is like your surname. The descriptive name (which is like your Christian name or forename) that follows describes some aspect of the fish – in this example, *bicolor*, meaning 'two colours', refers to the brown or black body and the bright red tail.

'Plecostomus' (*Hypostomus sp.*): bottom fish

Red-tailed black shark (*Labeo bicolor*)

Live-bearing Species

Tropical fish fall into two basic categories: 'live-bearers', that is, those fish which give birth to fully formed young; and 'egg-layers', where, after fertilization, the eggs hatch and may or may not be looked after by the parents.

The guppy (*Poecilia reticulata*)
This is one of the most popular aquarium fish because it is attractive, easy to keep and inexpensive to buy. The male is colourful, the female drab. There are many beautiful species to choose from. The guppy is a shoaling fish that will grow to about 4 cm ($1\frac{1}{2}$ in) in length and is quite at home in a temperature range of about 18°–26°C (65°–80°F).

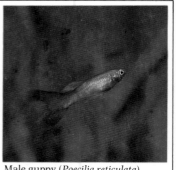
Male guppy (*Poecilia reticulata*)

The swordtail (*Xiphophorus helleri*)
This colourful fish is native to Central America. The male has the lower rays of its caudal fin extended, creating the 'sword'. Male swordtails are sometimes aggressive and quarrel with one another. Females are larger than the males and may grow to about 9 cm ($3\frac{1}{2}$ in) long. The native colour of this species is green, but red, black and many mixed-colour varieties have been bred.

The platy (*Xiphophorus maculatus*)
The platy originates in Southern Mexico, Guatemala and Honduras. It is a peaceful, sociable fish, well suited to community life in the aquarium. They come in a wide range of colours and can be reliable and easy breeders. The platy appreciates hard, alkaline water, and its pre-ferred temperature is probably between 24° and 26°C (75° and 80°F). The aquarium should also be well lit, so as to provide enough algae for their needs.

Green swordtail (*Xiphophorus helleri*)

The mollies (*Poecilia sphenops* and other species)
The mollies are popular live-bearers. They are green and gold spotted or all black, depending on which species you have – there are about six species available. One problem

Platy (*Xiphophorus maculatus*)

when breeding them is that they are often raised in brackish water and do not always re-adjust to fresh water. In the wild, they live in fresh or brackish waters in Central and northern South America.

Mollies (*Poecilia velifera*)

Egg-laying Species

Most tropical fish are egg-layers – which you choose depends very much on your personal taste.

The barbs

These are popular and colourful fish, named after the tiny barbels that are around their mouths (although not all barbs have barbels). They come from South-east Asia and many of the outlying islands, as well as Africa and Asia. Some species are fully grown at 2.5 cm (1 in) long; others, in the wild, grow to more than 1 m (3 ft). Most of the species commonly available, however, will not reach more than 5 or 6 cm (2–2½ in) in length. They have no teeth in the jaws but use bones in the throat for chewing.

The rasboras

Natives of South-east Asia, the rasboras are sociable fish, best displayed in small shoals. A few species breed easily in aquaria and most of the commonly available varieties will thrive on flake food.

The cichlids

Cichlids come from South America and Africa and include the very popular angelfish (*Pterophyllum scalare*) from South America. The original wild species had an olive-brown body with dark vertical bars, but there are

Barbus pentazona

Rasbora reticulata

now mottled, albino and 'blusher' varieties with variously exaggerated fin lengths. All of these have been produced, mostly in the Far East, by selective breeding, using the fishes' natural genetic variability. Recently, however, some unscrupulous exporters have been sending over angelfish which have been injected with coloured dyes. These fish, which can be recognized by their coloured patches, should be avoided at all costs and their import discouraged, as the mortality rate is high. Angelfish, especially when small, are a graceful addition to any aquarium. Beware, though, as larger ones do tend to eat smaller fish. Well-matched pairs will breed easily and look after their young.

The colourful 'mbuna' from Lake Malawi are popular, but unsuitable for the home aquarium as they are markedly territorial.

The corydoras
The corydoras come from South America and are jolly, cheerful little fish that rummage around the bottom of the tank, picking up leftover food and taking edible material out of the detritus. They are small fish, and often prettily marked with spots, stripes or a bronzy iridescent sheen. In a community tank they are almost essential because of their valuable function as refuse collectors.

Angelfish (*Pterophyllum scalare*)

Corydoras aeneus

Picking out Healthy Stock

It is extremely important to start off with healthy stock, otherwise your fish will be very short-lived. The standard of supplies of live fish varies enormously, so if possible talk to experienced aquarists and get their advice on who are the best suppliers in your area.

As a general rule, a shop that sells only fish is more likely to be a better choice than one that sells all kinds of pets. The size of the shop is immaterial: some very small establishments may keep fish that are healthier and better-quarantined than much larger places. A shop that specifically states that all its fish are quarantined is better than one that does not. Look especially for tanks labelled 'Not for Sale – Fish in Quarantine'. This means, hopefully, that any diseases imported with the fish will not be present in those finally sold to the customer.

Sometimes, however, in less reputable fish emporia, you may find such notices on some of the aquaria but you may also notice that the water is continually circulating from one tank to the next, thereby transferring any ailments throughout the entire stock of fish. So use your eyes. And take advice.

Once you have chosen your supplier, look at the other inmates of the tanks which contain the fish you want: if there are any unhealthy fish, do not buy. It is also wise not to buy fish from very dirty tanks. Those with very unhealthy occupants (i.e. dead) must obviously be avoided.

A healthy fish will be active (save the nocturnal and naturally sedentary varieties), with erect fins and a smooth skin, and will generally be pursuing fish activities.

One final warning: many diseased fish do not show obvious signs of illness, so, especially if you are introducing new fish into an already established aquarium of healthy fish, keep the newcomers separate for a while. Despite all precautions, experience dictates that you should prepare yourself for deaths, although we hope these will be few.

General signs of unhealthiness
Sunken bellies
Protruding scales
Listlessness (except in some retiring or
  nocturnal fish)
Discoloured patches on the skin
Ragged fins
White spots
White strands like cotton wool
Milky eyes (where applicable)
Irregular swimming or an irregular
  position (though some catfish,
  amongst others, naturally rest at
  'peculiar' angles)

Black molly with white spot disease

Aquaria

Tank size

Aquaria come in a wide range of types and designs, to suit all tastes and pockets. They are made in various combinations of materials (Perspex or glass, with or without iron frames). The lightest modern aquaria are made of glass sealed with silicone glue.

Do remember that a tank full of water is very heavy, so it is important to make sure that the bottom of even a lightweight aquarium is fully supported on a complete and firm base.

Unless you need an aquarium for a specialized purpose, such as an infirmary or as a rearing or quarantine tank, *never* get one less than 45 cm long, 30 cm wide and 30 cm deep (18 × 12 × 12 in). As a general rule no measurement should ever be less than the depth. Bow-fronted aquaria cost a lot more than the rectangular ones and do little to enhance the quality of life for the fish.

Avoid overcrowding

To work out how many fish may safely be kept in an unaerated tank, the rule is 2.5 cm (1 in) of fish body length per 4.5 litres (1 gallon) of water. For example, a 60 × 30 × 30 cm (24 × 12 × 12 in) tank holding 45 litres (10 gallons) of water can accommodate approximately 25 cm (10 in) of fishes.

Aeration

Although an aerator is not strictly necessary, the number of fish a tank is able to accommodate is greatly increased – almost doubled – by aeration.

Position

It is best to keep an aquarium away from extremes of temperature and also out of continuous bright light, so a window sill is not a good place. Look for a spot away from direct sunlight or a room heater – an alcove beside a chimney breast is often a good place.

Feeding hole cover

Home from home In setting up your aquarium you should aim to copy the conditions that your fish like in the wild. For example, shy, nocturnal fish will want rocks to hide beneath, while other, more adventurous fish will need planty of open water.

Water In different parts of Britain the nature of the water varies between soft and hard, acid or alkaline. Kits are available to help you check the quality of water for hardness and for the pH (degree of acidity or alkalinity). Chlorine (a gas added by the Water Board to sterilize drinking water) levels vary, too, and these can affect your fish. Before introducing fish to your aquarium, allow the water in the tank to stand for a few days so that the chlorine escapes. For some fish rainwater is preferable. Make sure it is collected in a clean container and, again, allow it to stand for several days before putting it in the tank. Usually rainwater is softer than domestic water.

Remember, too, that in a heated aquarium – even one with a lid on – water constantly evaporates. Evaporation will concentrate the minerals in the water and each time you top up, especially with tap water, the mineral concentration will increase. For this reason it's a good plan to top up with distilled water.

Heating You will need to heat your aquarium because even in houses with central heating the average temperature is too low for most tropical fish. You can buy separate or combined heaters and thermostats. A simple and effective arrangement is to place the heater near the filter or air source, and the thermostat the other side of the tank. The water current will circulate the heat and the thermostat will control it. *Please obey the instructions on wiring up the heater and thermostat very carefully. Water and electricity are a dangerous mixture for both you and the fish.*

Filter An aerator or pump, as already mentioned, is not essential but is useful, especially if combined with a filter. The filter may be a simple plastic box, through which air enters the tank. The currents thereby set up trap detritus in the fibreglass wool in the filter. A useful tip is to place a layer of activated charcoal between two layers of fibreglass wool, as this will absorb many of the accumulating organic products from fish excretion which can inhibit fish growth.

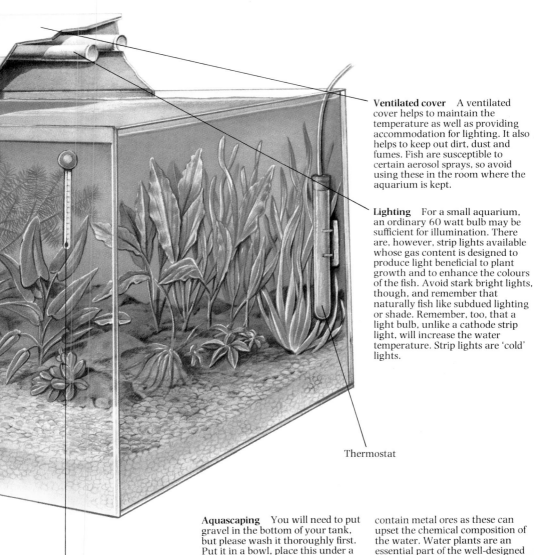

Ventilated cover A ventilated cover helps to maintain the temperature as well as providing accommodation for lighting. It also helps to keep out dirt, dust and fumes. Fish are susceptible to certain aerosol sprays, so avoid using these in the room where the aquarium is kept.

Lighting For a small aquarium, an ordinary 60 watt bulb may be sufficient for illumination. There are, however, strip lights available whose gas content is designed to produce light beneficial to plant growth and to enhance the colours of the fish. Avoid stark bright lights, though, and remember that naturally fish like subdued lighting or shade. Remember, too, that a light bulb, unlike a cathode strip light, will increase the water temperature. Strip lights are 'cold' lights.

Thermostat

Thermometer

Aquascaping You will need to put gravel in the bottom of your tank, but please wash it thoroughly first. Put it in a bowl, place this under a running tap and keep stirring the gravel until the water that flows out is quite clear. Rocks are an attractive and useful addition to your aquarium because algae will grow on them and fish can hide beneath them. Do avoid rocks like limestone, though, or those that contain metal ores as these can upset the chemical composition of the water. Water plants are an essential part of the well-designed aquarium (see page 20). Not only are they visually pleasing, but they also perform several useful functions: they put oxygen into the water; they provide cover for the fish and a surface for egg-laying; and they provide a source of food for some species.

Butterfly fish (*Pantodon buchholtzi*)

Ruby barb (*Barbus nigrofasciatus*)

Cardinal tetras (*Cheirodon axelrodi*)

Red swordtail (*Xiphophorus helleri*)

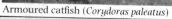

Armoured catfish (*Corydoras paleatus*)

Flying fox (*Epalzeorhynchus kallopterus*)

Stocking your Aquarium

There are a great number of ways in which you can stock and furnish your aquarium. The vital things to remember are to choose fish that are mutually compatible, and not to overstock your tank. Three schemes are suggested here which would make a well-balanced aquarium and which would provide both a congenial environment for the fish and an attractive moving picture of colour and light. All the schemes are based on a tank $60 \times 30 \times 30$ cm ($24 \times 12 \times 12$ in).

Scheme No. 1

This is suitable for a tank in a hard and alkaline water area.

Black molly (*Poecilia sphenops*)

Fish
5 tiger barbs (*Barbus tetrazona*)
2 pairs black mollies (*Poecilia sphenops*)
2 pairs guppies (*Poecilia reticulata*)
1 pair swordtails (*Xiphophorus helleri*)
1 pair pearl gourami (*Trichogaster leeri*)
2–3 corydoras (*Corydoras aeneus* or *paleatus*)
1 Siamese 'algae' eater (*Gyrinocheilus aymonieri*)
2 small angelfish (*Pterophyllum scalare*)

Plants
Select plants of varying heights (with the tallest at the back and the shortest in the front). Approximately two dozen would be a good number, although this will depend on how much other tank decoration (rocks, stones, bogwood, etc.) you include. Choose from any of the plants listed below:
Echinodorus paniculatus (Amazon Swordplant)
Sagittaria
Vallisneria
Ludwigia (Swamp Loosestrife)
Hygrophila

Tiger barbs (*Barbus tetrazona*)

Scheme No. 2

This is suitable for a tank situated in an area of less hard water than referred to in Scheme 1.

Fish
5 tiger barbs (*Barbus tetrazona*)
5 cardinal tetras (*Cheirodon axelrodi*)
5 glowlight tetras (*Hemmigrammus erythrozonus*)
2 pairs guppies (*Poecilia reticulata*)
1 pair pearl gourami (*Trichogaster leeri*)
2 corydoras (*Corydoras aeneus* or *paleatus*)
1 Siamese 'algae' eater (*Gyrinocheilus aymonieri*)
2 small angelfish (*Pterophyllum scalare*)
5 zebra fish (*Brachydanio rerio*)

Plants
Choose from any of the suggestions in Scheme 1, plus:
Cryptocorynes
Acorus
Cabomba
Ceratopteris

Kissing gourami (*Helostoma temmincki*)

Scheme No. 3

Fish
5 glass catfish (*Kryptopterus bicirrhis*)
5 glowlight tetras (*Hemmigrammus erythrozonus*)
1 Siamese fighting fish (*Betta splendens*)
2 kissing gourami (*Helostoma temmincki*)
2–3 corydoras (*Corydoras aeneus* or *paleatus*)
1 'plecostomus' (*Hypostomus sp.*)
3 harlequins (*Rasbora heteromorpha*)
2 pairs guppies (*Poecilia reticulata*)

Plants
Select any of the plants from Schemes 1 and 2, according to the quality of your water.

Water Plants

Water plants are one of the most attractive – and important – aspects of a well-planned aquarium. They come in many sizes and shapes, from bushy growths that hide the corners of the tank, to slender waving fronds that look pretty and give shelter for baby fish. Plants put vital oxygen into the water, too, as well as providing food for some vegetarian fish and hiding places for others. They can also help to reduce algae problems.

Water plants can sometimes be difficult to grow as certain species require specific water conditions and lighting. However, artificial water plants are also available and these can provide some greenery in the aquarium until the live plants become established.

For hard water areas *Echinodorus paniculatus* (Amazon Swordplant) is a popular choice. It comes in two varieties, one with narrow and one with broad leaves, and is fairly easy to propagate, too. *Vallisneria* is a slim-leaved plant which is good for producing shade at the back and sides of the tank, and is found in several different varieties. *Elodea* (waterweed or Canadian pondweed) is a rapid grower and provides shade as well as food for some fish. *Sagittaria*, with its broad leaves, is another swift-growing plant and a very useful oxygenator.

For areas where the water is softer, try *Cryptocoryne* species. They are excellent foreground plants and very decorative, but tend to be rather slow growers. They vary in size and are good where the light is weak. *Ludwigia* (Swamp Loosestrife) is often a good choice as it grows quickly, is decorative and because its leaves provide useful food. The attractive *Cabomba* is another good oxygenator, useful at the sides and back of the tank.

Most plants, of course, have roots and therefore a suitable coarse sand or gravel (thoroughly washed: see page 15) should be provided for them so that they can grow. Some aquatic plants, however, have a weak root structure and may be sold with a small band of lead (harmless to fish) around their bases to keep them weighted down.

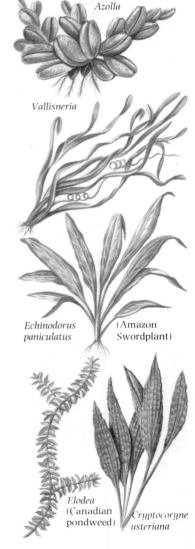

Azolla

Vallisneria

Echinodorus paniculatus   (Amazon Swordplant)

Elodea (Canadian pondweed)   Cryptocoryne usteriana

Settling in Your Fish

Getting the aquarium ready

Once you have set up your aquarium in its permanent position, planted your plants, and tested out your heating, lighting and filtration system, it is advisable to wait a week or two before you introduce your fish. This gives the plants a chance to get established, enables the water to 'age', and offers you the opportunity to make sure everything is working just as it should.

Bringing home your fish

Having bought your fish, the next step is to bring them safely home. They will most likely be in plastic bags. If you have a long journey, ask the shop assistant to put the plastic bags in a polystyrene container so that the temperature loss is kept to a minimum. Normally the supplier will ensure that enough air is contained above the water in each bag for the fish to survive: the bag must contain slightly more air than water, and the fish should not be crowded.

Introducing the fish to your aquarium

It is important to remember that fish cannot adapt to sudden changes in temperature, so you need to make sure that the temperature of the water in the plastic bag containing your fish is equal to that in the aquarium. Leave the fish inside the bag in the tank for an hour or two to equalize the water temperatures. Turn the light off, as the bag might touch the bulb and melt, causing problems. When the moment comes for their release into the aquarium, slowly undo or cut the bag and let the fish swim out of their own accord.

You might find it best to keep the light off to begin with while the fish explore their new surroundings, but then turn it on and feed them. Healthy fish enjoy eating, so being given a meal after what has been for them a traumatic experience, can help to settle them down and encourage them to associate their new environment with a regular supply of food.

To transport your fish, place the plastic bag inside a polystyrene container to maintain water temperature

Feeding

Fish soon learn about food. If you feed them at, say, 7 p.m. each evening, before that time they will be waiting below the spot at which the food is introduced. Regular times for meals are a sensible idea for you and the fish.

A well-balanced diet
Most of the proprietary flake foods will be suitable for almost all fish. They have the advantage of containing appropriate amounts of minerals, vitamins, fats and fibres, and are also convenient to dispense. You will need to judge the quantity carefully for yourself, but as a general rule of thumb *don't give fish more food than they can eat in a couple of minutes.* It is better to feed a little and often, rather than too much at one go. Excess food is not always eaten later: it simply pollutes the water and increases the bacteria content and the subsequent risk of disease.

Live food is always beneficial
The most commonly available are small crustaceans called *Daphnia*, or water fleas, which can be put into the tank straightaway. You can also get live blood worms (the larvae of mosquito-like insects) and tubifex worms. Be wary of tubifex worms, however, as although they are a good and nutritious food, they live half-buried in possibly disease-carrying mud, in foul, low-oxygen-content waters.

Household foods can be included in the menu
A few ordinary household foods are good for fish, but always give them in *small* quantities mixed with proprietary brands. Finely chopped lean meat and ground fish are worth adding to the diet, and so are ground porridge oats and some of the invalid foods. Very small fish (newly born young or dwarf species) will benefit from small quantities of finely crumbled up hard-boiled egg yolks. Vegetarian fish will appreciate small pieces of lettuce leaf in their diet.

Water fleas (*Daphnia*)

Tubifex worms Keep tubifex worms in a bowl under a trickling cold tap for at least three days before you feed them to your fish. Without the mud they knot their bodies into a ball, so you will lose only the dead ones, and the process will rid the rest of any disease they may be carrying.

Maintenance and Handling

Scraping off excess algae

The well-run aquarium

A well-established aquarium will almost run itself. You may need to scrape off excess algae from time to time, but take care when scraping the sides of plastic tanks or you will badly scratch them. Snails are helpful in keeping the aquarium clean for they feed on algae. You will also need to clean it out occasionally, especially if you have provided a filter which accumulates the detritus. If you have to do this, carefully catch your fish and place them in a *covered* container in water of the same temperature. Transfer the plants to a bowl of water and switch off the electricity supply. Scoop out the water and then the rocks and gravel. Never attempt to carry an aquarium with water and/or rocks in it. It will be very heavy and the bottom of the tank could easily crack. Wash the gravel under running water and clean out the tank carefully. Then replace the gravel, fill up with water (if from the tap, let it stand to lose the chlorine), replace the plants, heater, etc., and finally, when the temperature is right, reintroduce your fish.

Safe and sensible handling

Fish are delicate and sensitive creatures. Careless handling can easily hurt them, and so can abrupt changes in temperature or light and strong vibrations, like sudden loud noises or tapping on the side of the tank.

In general, fish must not be handled with your bare hands at all, for the reasons explained on page 4. If you must move them to temporary accommodation, it is best to use a net to catch them. In these circumstances, do remember to equalize the water temperatures as outlined on page 21.

It is not a good idea to plunge fish abruptly from bright light into sudden darkness or vice versa. If you have a lit aquarium try to remember to turn the light off before the room lights at night, so as to make the transition to darkness gentler and more gradual for the fish.

Always use a net to catch fish

Ailments

Fish ailments and diseases are very hard to diagnose as superficially similar symptoms may be caused by many different infections. Bacteria, fungi, viruses, protozoa (single-celled organisms) and helminths (internal parasites or worms) can all affect fish. So can adverse environmental factors, over which we may have a certain degree of control.

Too rapid temperature change
If a tropical fish is suddenly placed in water that is too cold, it will go into a state of shock (as it will if the heater or thermostat fails). This is manifest in a slow, weaving style of swimming often called shimmying. Too rapid a rise in temperature will cause a shortage of oxygen in the water so that the fish will gasp for breath at the surface.

Poisons
Many of the heavy metals are poisonous to tropical fish. Of these, the worst is copper, so you must avoid having copper in contact with aquarium water. Zinc can also be lethal. Lead, although a poison, is less of a problem (for instance, if used to weight down aquatic plants) because it rapidly becomes covered by a layer of inert lead oxide.

Other ordinary substances are deleterious to fish health. Aerosol sprays should not be used in close proximity to the aquarium. Insecticides can be lethal.

Bad feeding
Complaints due to incorrect feeding may not appear immediately. By the time that something is seen to be wrong, it may be too late. Too much of one type of food can cause intestinal troubles (flake food, however, is mixed) and too much fat and carbohydrate in the diet can lead to degeneration of the digestive organs and the deposition of unhealthy fat. Should your fish have persistent long strings of faeces, something is wrong: try changing the diet.

Diseases

There are other complaints fish suffer from, which are to some extent outside your control.

White spot disease (*Ichthyophthirius*)
This is a fairly common disease caused by protozoa. The skin of the fish becomes covered by small white spots about the size of a pin head. The damaging organism is called *Ichthyophthirius*, often abbreviated to 'ick'. Ick matures in the skin of the fish where it feeds on skin cells. It then leaves the fish and reproduces. The hundreds of young in their turn feed on the fish, thereby continuing the cycle.

As fish can be infected before the white spots are visible, quarantining new fish before introducing them to the tank is very important.

Fungus
Fungus is a general term for several different infections that show up as cotton wool-like stands on the fish's body, fins and gills. If left untreated, fungus can be fatal.

Basic treatment
Isolate any suspect fish as quickly as possible, to avoid the spread of disease. Treatments for white spot, fungus and many other diseases are available from good aquarium shops, but don't expect universal success. There is nothing wrong with many of the medicaments: the problem is that similar symptoms arise from different causes.

There are various chemicals available that can prevent many diseases, but you would be well advised to read widely before using them as, incorrectly applied, they can do more harm than good.

Rules for health
Choose strong healthy fish. Keep them in clean conditions. Feed them wisely. If you follow these basic rules, with luck your fish will die only of old age.

If you have a sick fish, try to isolate it at once, either by putting it in a separate aquarium (a sick tank or infirmary) or by floating a jam jar of aquarium water in the aquarium with the patient therein.

The Healthy Tropical Fish

Appetite	good, with food eaten swiftly and with enthusiasm.
Breathing	gill covers rise and fall rhythmically; gulping at the surface (except in the case of labyrinth fish, loaches and some catfish) indicates oxygen starvation.
Demeanour	alert; one fish which leaves the rest of its shoal to be by itself may be sick.
Eyes	usually bright and clear.
Fins	entire, without tears, splits, white spot or streaks of blood; should be held away from the body; not drooping or folded.
Position in water	swimming freely; sick fish may sink to the bottom or float on the surface on their side (although catfish especially often adopt seemingly odd positions).
Scales	scales should show no injury or fungal growth; protruding scales are a sign of disease.
Vent	clean, no trailing faeces.

Different species of tropical fish require different conditions, both of temperature and of habitat. However, certain common rules of health apply to them all and it's sensible to observe your fish with these guidelines in mind.

Home Aquarium Checklist

1	Talk to expert aquarists and get some ideas.
2	Decide on the site, size, content and cost of your tank.
3	Investigate heating and lighting systems.
4	Purchase tank, stand, cover, heater, thermostat, thermometer, gravel, plants, etc.
5	Thoroughly wash gravel.
6	Clean tank inside and out and put in its permanent site.
7	Add gravel, rocks and other decorations and half fill the tank with water.
8	Put in your plants and complete the aquascaping.
9	Add heater, thermostat (following the manufacturer's instructions), thermometer and aerator (if used). Do not connect to mains.
10	Fill tank, leaving air space below cover.
11	Connect heating system to the mains and switch on, following the manufacturer's instructions.
12	Add cover and check lights.
13	Leave tank for at least one week. Make daily temperature checks. Keep an eye out for leaks.
14	Buy your fish. Make absolutely sure the ones you have chosen are compatible with one another.
15	Finally, add your fish to the tank.

Reproduction

Breeding conditions

You have already learned that fish can either give birth to live young or lay eggs, but it is very important to realize that different species require different conditions if they are to breed successfully. So, in a mixed tank, the breeding environment that might suit a guppy can be quite inappropriate for, say, a gourami.

For example, live-bearing fishes' young can survive in a heavily weeded community tank without any extra precautions, but egg-laying species require a multitude of different habitats: some scatter their eggs over gravel, into which they fall and subsequently develop unattended by their parents, while others, for example labyrinth fish such as gouramis and Siamese fighting fish, make bubble nests at the surface and protect them and the young carefully. Some cichlids and catfish lay sticky eggs onto rocks or plants and may or may not (depending on the species) look after the eggs and/or young, while other cichlids excavate nests for their eggs in the sand or gravel.

It is also important to remember that in the wild only a very small proportion of the fry born actually reach adulthood. This is substantially true in home aquarium conditions, too, as many of the young fry are eaten by other fish, including, very often, their own parents. In order to raise the maximum number of young, therefore, it may be necessary to isolate them from the other fish, either by using a separate nursery tank, or by putting in a divider or partition into your existing aquarium.

Fish breeding requires specialized knowledge

As you will by now appreciate, tropical fish breeding is a complex business and should not be entered into lightly. If you are intent on breeding your fish, it is strongly recommended that you talk to a number of experienced fish breeders and read a variety of reference books to gain more information and guidance on the subject.

Some cichlids guard their young carefully

The Beauty of Tropical Fish

This section describes a small selection of attractive fish with which you could stock your aquarium.

Zebra fish (*Brachydanio rerio*)
A native of India, this fish enjoys a water temperature between 20° and 23°C (68° and 73°F). A very active and lively fish, it will reach a size of about 5 cm (2 in) and is best kept in shoals.

Glass catfish (*Kryptopterus bicirrhis*)
An almost transparent catfish – you can see its bones. It originates in South-east Asia and grows to about 10 cm (4 in) long. It enjoys a temperature range of 21°–26°C (70°–80°F), and is generally an active, free-swimming, shoaling fish.

Siamese fighting fish (*Betta splendens*)
This is a hardy species, but you must have only one male in a tank otherwise fighting will break out. If you want to see it display itself, put a mirror at the side of the tank.

Zebra fish (*Brachydanio rerio*)

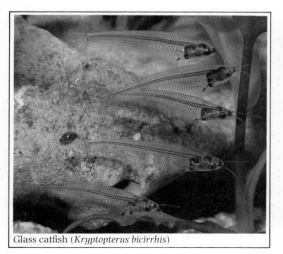

Glass catfish (*Kryptopterus bicirrhis*)

Siamese fighting fish (*Betta splendens*)

Harlequin (*Rasbora heteromorpha*)

Harlequin (*Rasbora heteromorpha*)
A lively but peaceful rasbora which enjoys being in shoals, when all the fish move as one. It grows to a size of about 4.5 cm ($1\frac{3}{4}$ in) and appreciates soft, slightly acid water. The harlequin is an active and tolerant fish.

Siamese 'algae' eater (*Gyrinocheilus aymonieri*)
A fish that often becomes rather robust with age. It enjoys dense plant clumps, rocks and roots, which provide hiding places. It reaches a size of 15 cm (6 in) and enjoys a water temperature of around 25°C (77°F). Its common name is rather misleading, in fact, because it feeds on detritus more than algae.

Pearl gourami (*Trichogaster leeri*)
Very pretty fish, generally peaceful but sensitive to bad water conditions. They are best kept in pairs and will grow to a size of about 10 cm (4 in). They enjoy subdued light and algae. Pearl gourami build bubble nests in which they place their eggs.

Siamese 'algae' eater (*Gyrinocheilus aymonieri*)

Pearl gourami (*Trichogaster leeri*)

Index